ENTER THE DRAGON
SCRAPBOOK SEQUENCES VOLUME 14

Welcome to the thrilling journey through time and motion as we present the 13th instalment of the Bruce Lee Scrapbook Sequences. In this edition, we delve deeper into the mesmerizing world behind and in front of the camera, capturing fleeting moments of the legendary Bruce Lee's dynamism.

As you flip through these pages, you will witness a symphony of photographs taken in rapid succession, each frame encapsulating the lightning speed that defined Bruce Lee's unparalleled martial arts prowess. Beyond the kicks, punches, and graceful movements, this volume unveils the multifaceted persona of Bruce Lee as an actor.

Even when not in the throes of action, Bruce Lee's face became a canvas of emotions, offering a kaleidoscope of expressions. From his cheeky boyish smile that could light up a room to a countenance contorted with intense rage, every nuance is meticulously preserved within the confines of these pages. It is this wide range of emotions that elevated Bruce Lee from being just a martial artist to a captivating performer, leaving an indelible mark on the world of cinema.

In this fortunate 13th volume, we invite you to immerse yourself in the richness of Bruce Lee's legacy. May these sequences serve as a visual feast, allowing you to relive and appreciate the timeless charisma of a man who continues to inspire generations. Join us as we unravel the enigma.

The legend – BruceLee.

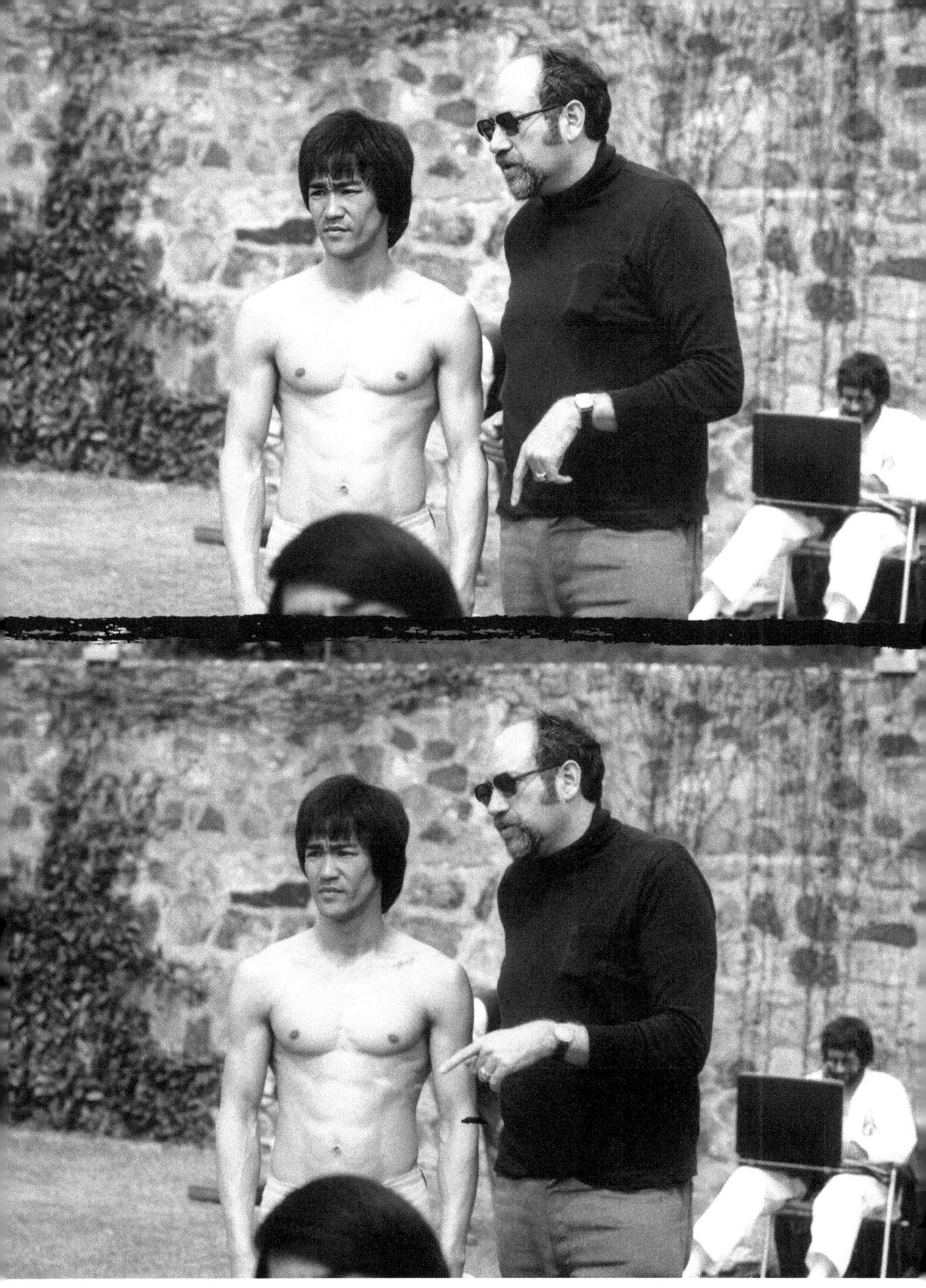

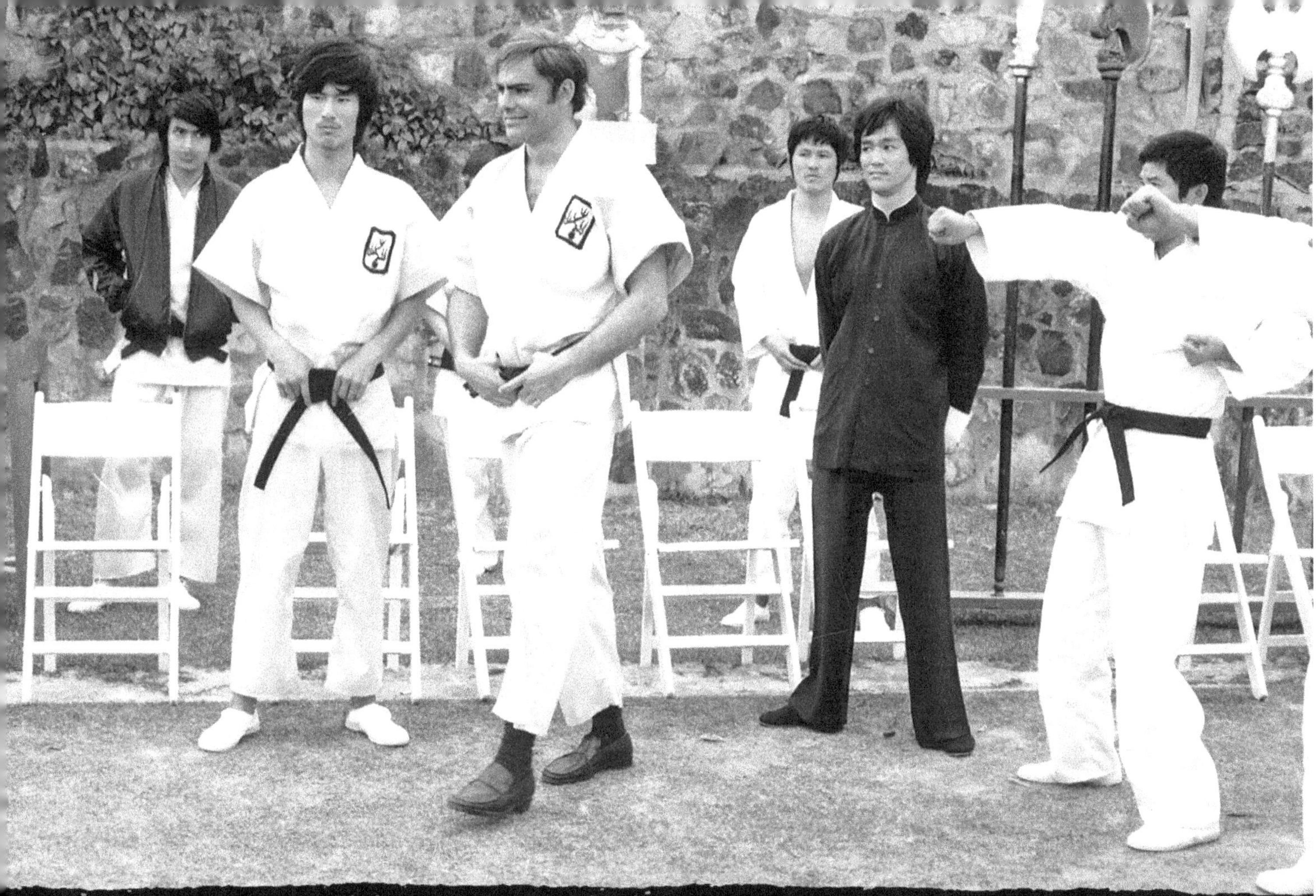

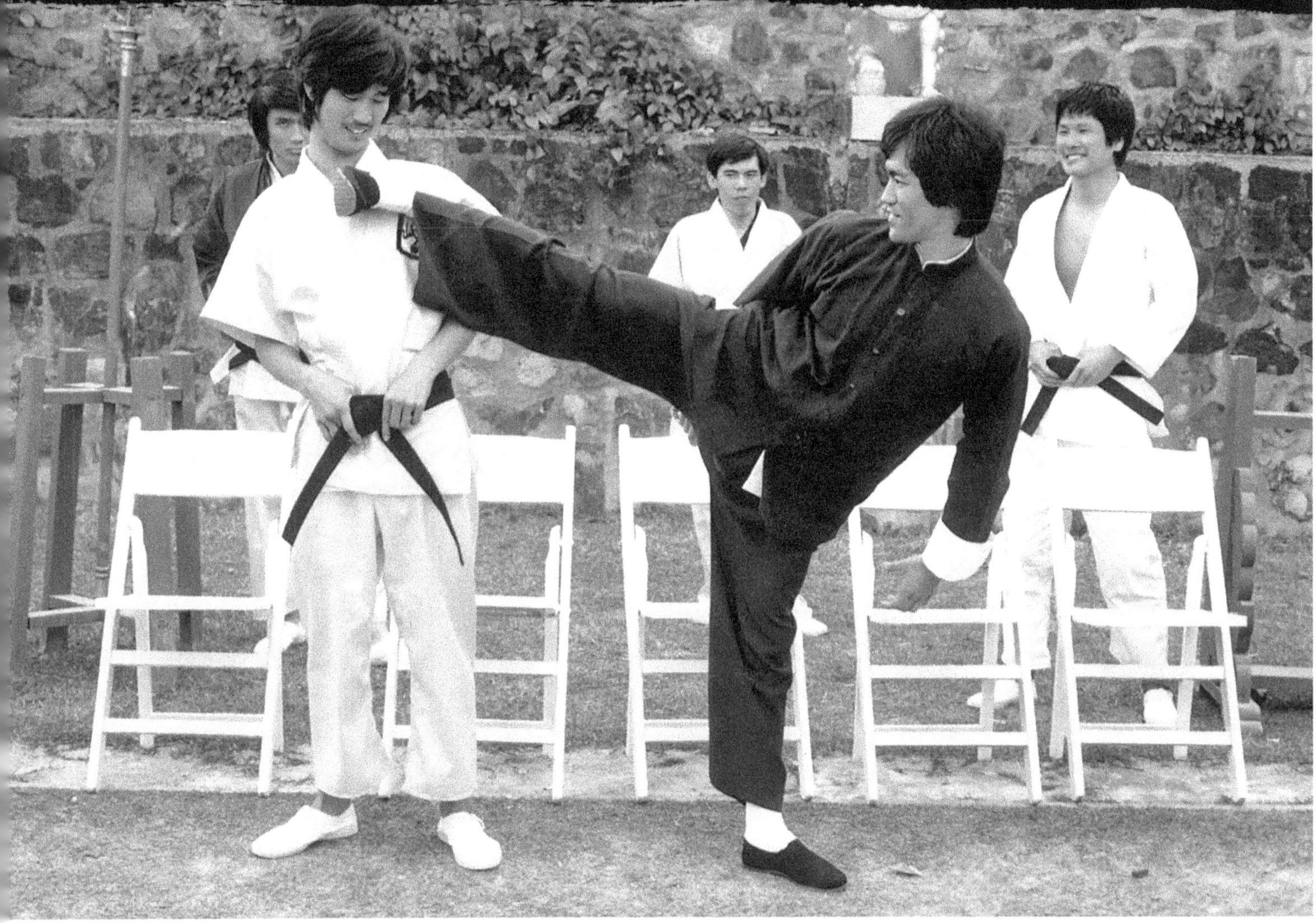

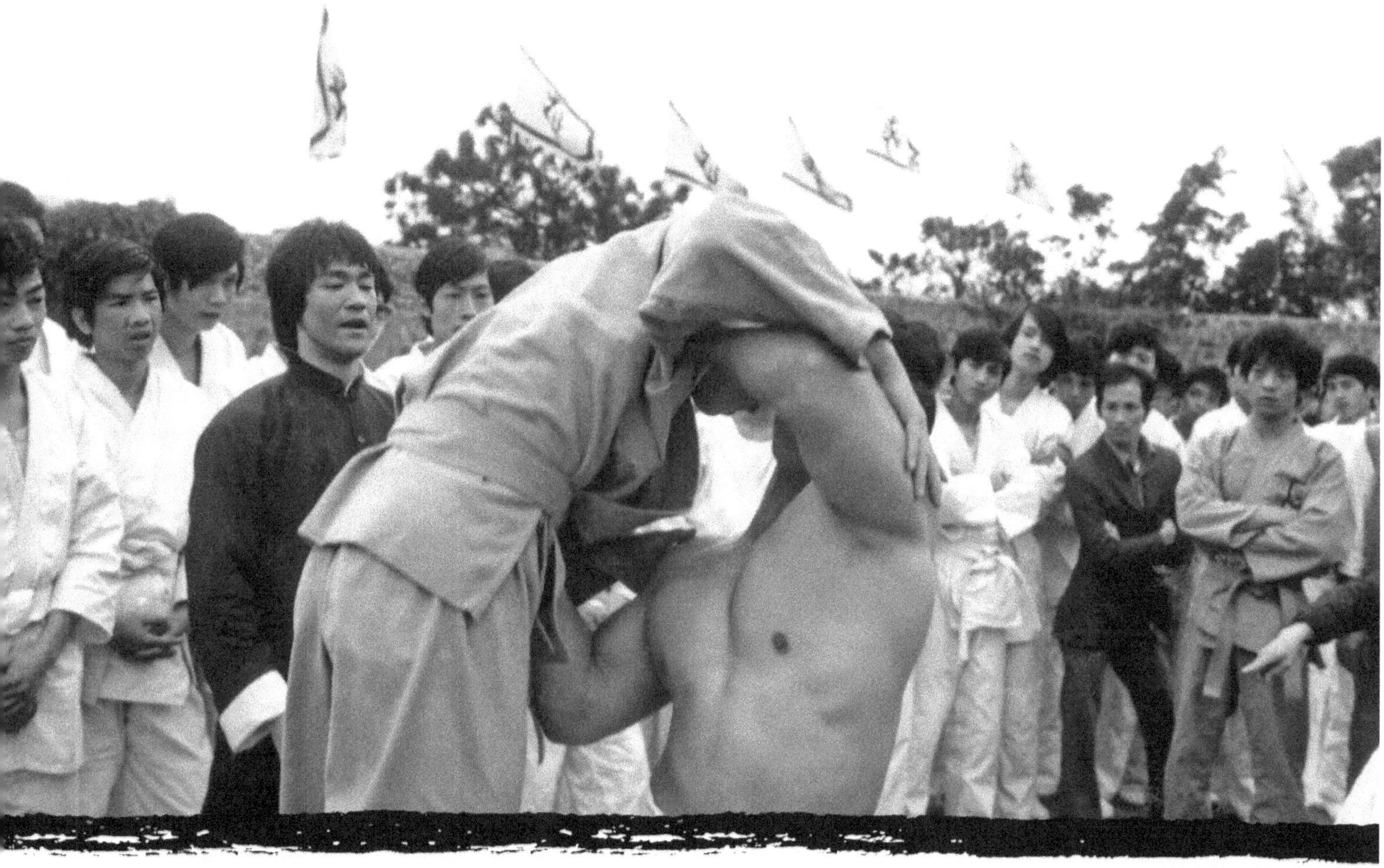

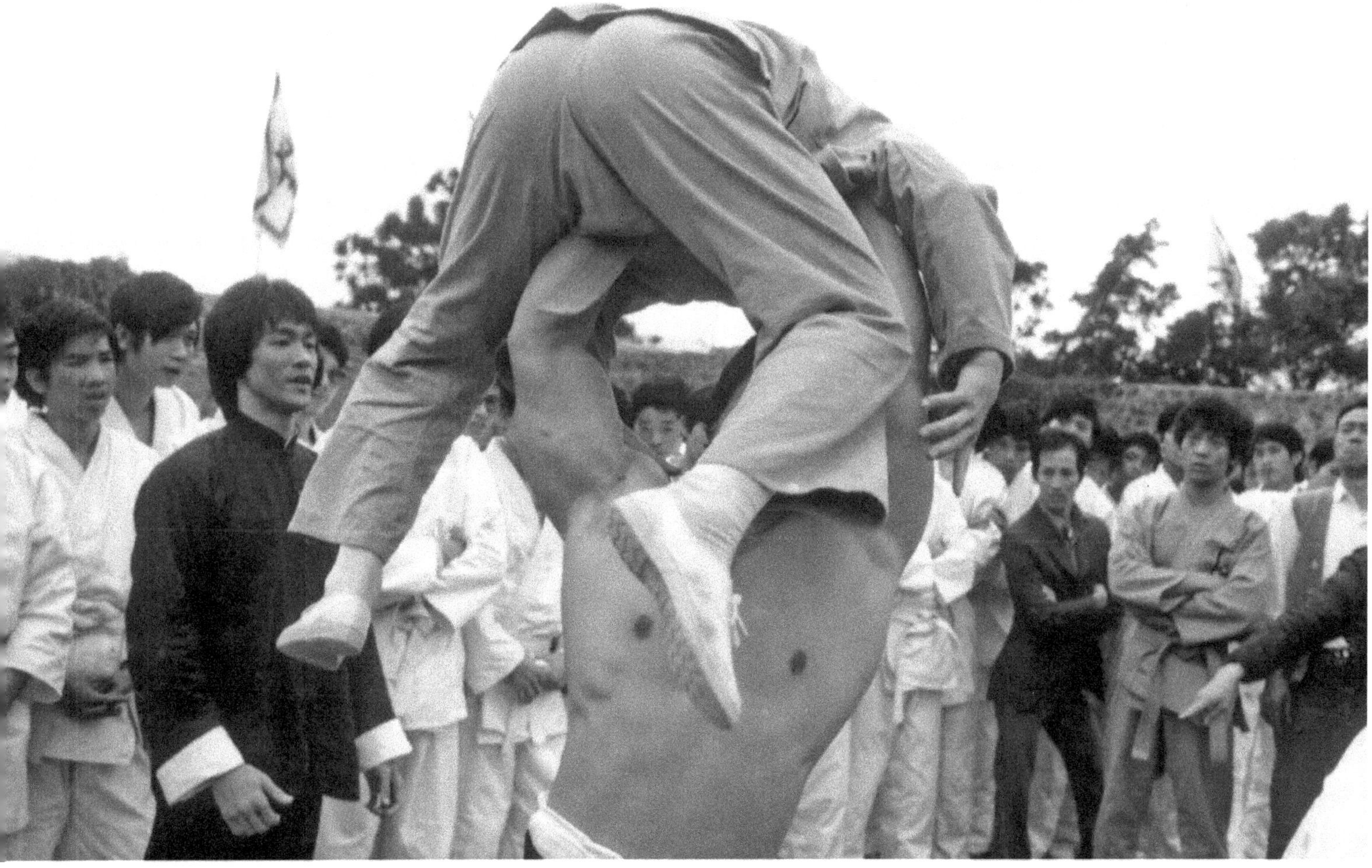

www.ingramcontent.com/pod-product-compliance
Lightning Source LLC
Chambersburg PA
CBHW061151010526
44118CB00026B/2943